INKTAIL

&

FRIENDS

Cedar Sanderson

Cover design by Cedar Sanderson, illustrations by Cedar Sanderson

FOREWORD:

This all started with a tiny dragon. I was doodling, and drew a little dragon peering shyly from behind a clump of wildflowers - Dodecatheon pulchellum, to be precise, commonly known as Shooting Star. One of my favorite spring flowers during my youth in Alaska, it was drawn for a friend who was just beginning her fight with breast cancer. Another friend complained that a small woodland in his hometown had been bulldozed and the stands of ladyslipper orchids and other wildflowers razed. I drew more little dragons with flowers. Fast forward, and I had all these little dragons in various activities, with no real idea of what I was going to do with them. Someone, and I can't remember who, asked if I was going to do a coloring book or a children's story.

I decided to do a coloring book. But I wanted one that would allow the coloring to extend beyond the lines, not be trapped into tiny repeating patterns. I wanted to create a coloring book that would encourage the coloring to become storytelling, to teach how to create and expand and learn. So I started keeping that in mind as I drew my little dragons. Now, you will see that not every page in this book is a dragon. And you'll find a simple tutorial at the end with an idea of how to begin to draw your own creatures. But the real secret is being willing to let go, don't try to make it perfect, and just have fun. Practice, study anatomy, and look at lots of pictures. Before you know it, you will truly be able to color outside the lines.

Happy Coloring!

Cedar Sanderson

Spring 2016

Coloring Tips:

For this book I suggest colored pencils to color the dragons and other creatures to best effect. When you begin, don't press down, just pull the pencil across the paper – the bottom of this page is a good place to try that out – and see how much pigment you put on the paper. A very light color lets you build slowly up, and blend other colors together with the first color, for pretty shading and many more colors than you may have in your set. I recommend nice colored pencils, not the cheapest, but you don't have to buy the most expensive, either. Your pigment will have richer colors and go further if you buy a nice set. But with the blending you can learn to get by with fewer colors.

Before you start coloring, you can create your own color wheel to learn your pencils better. Keep the inside of the wheel light and slowly darken toward the rim to practice shading. You can look up a color wheel if you want to see how to put the colors in, I've given you a little starting point but you can make it how you want.

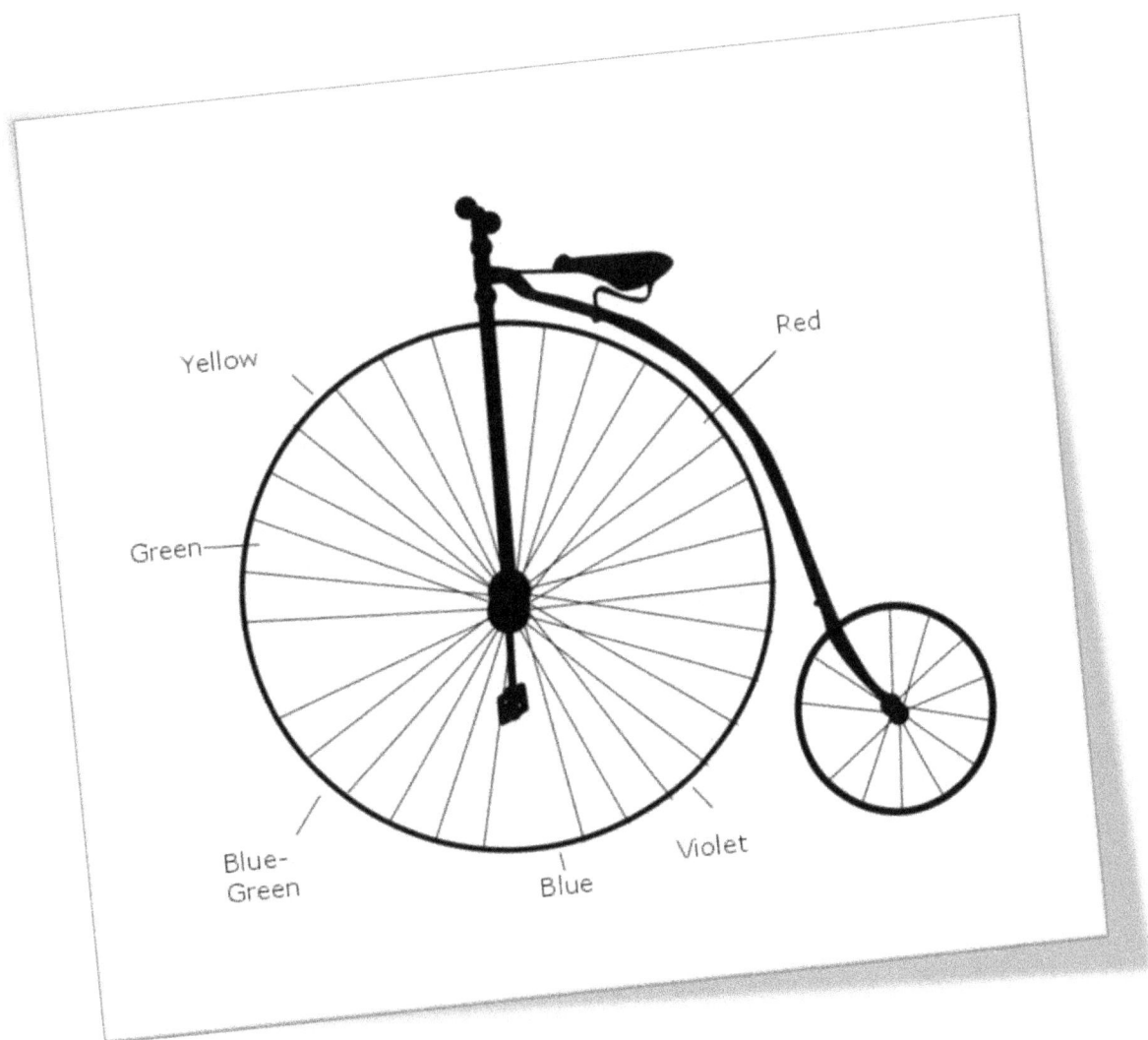

Yellow

Red

Green

Blue-
Green

Blue

Violet

INKTAIL AT WORK

PAGETURNER

CRUMPY BUNNY

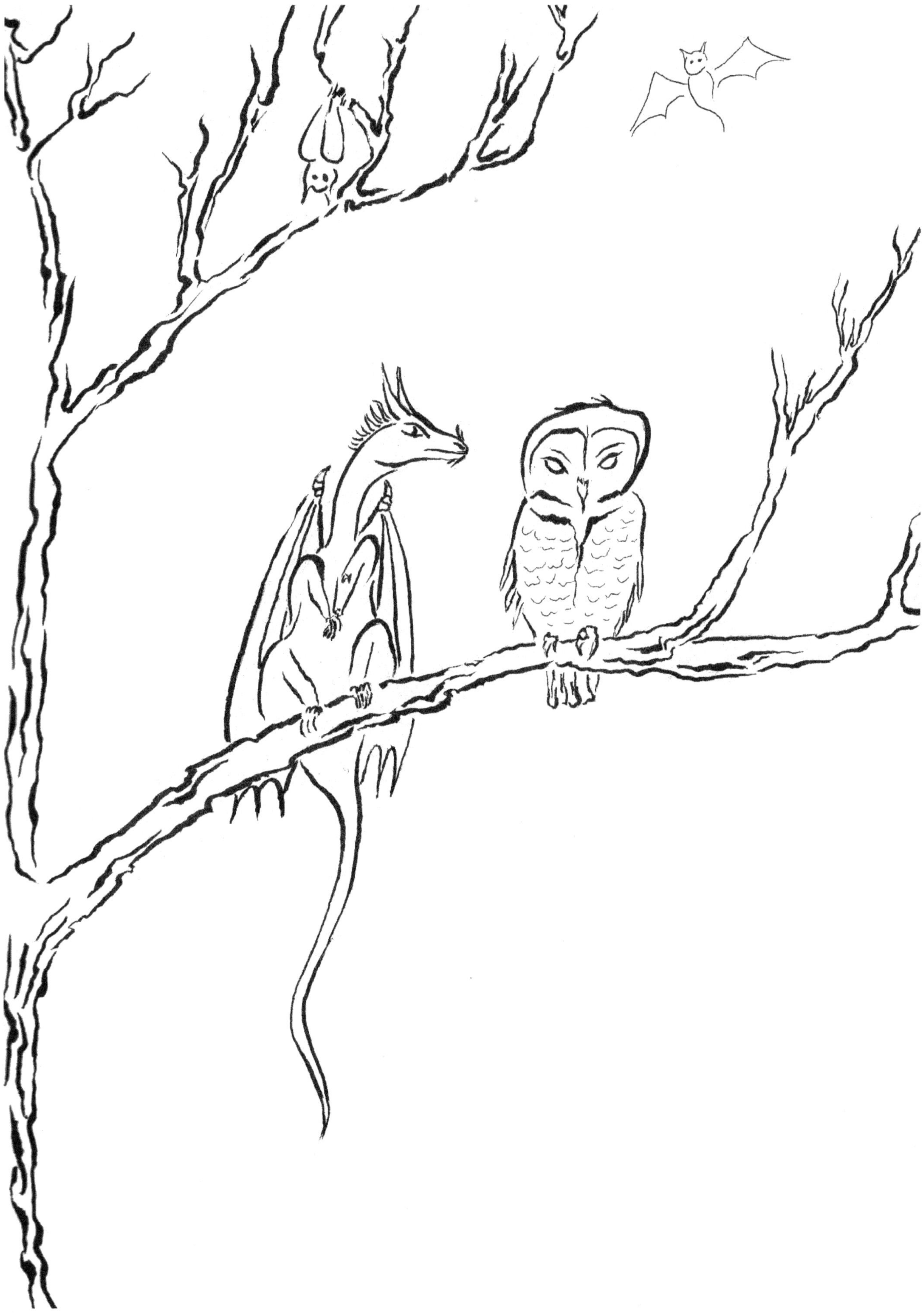

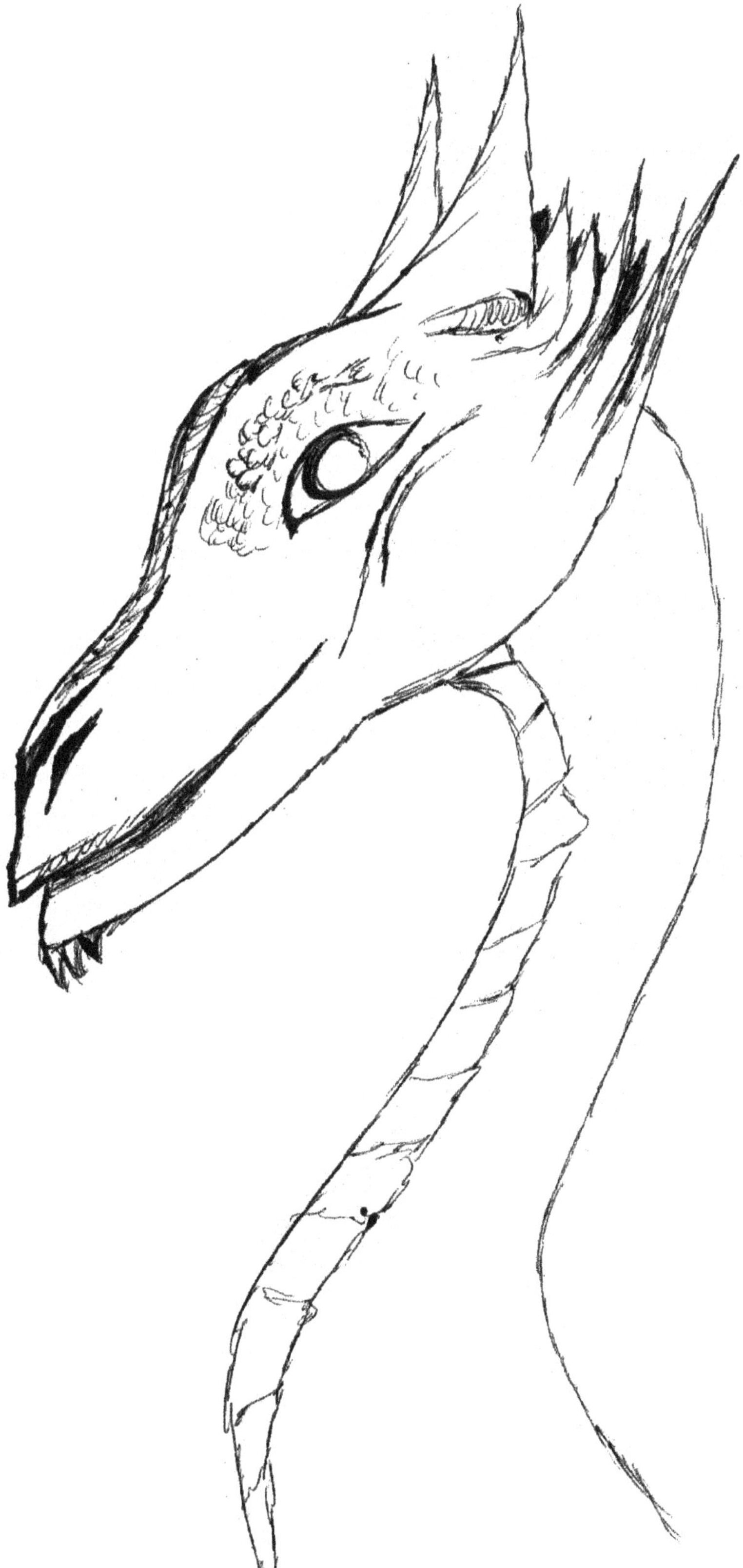

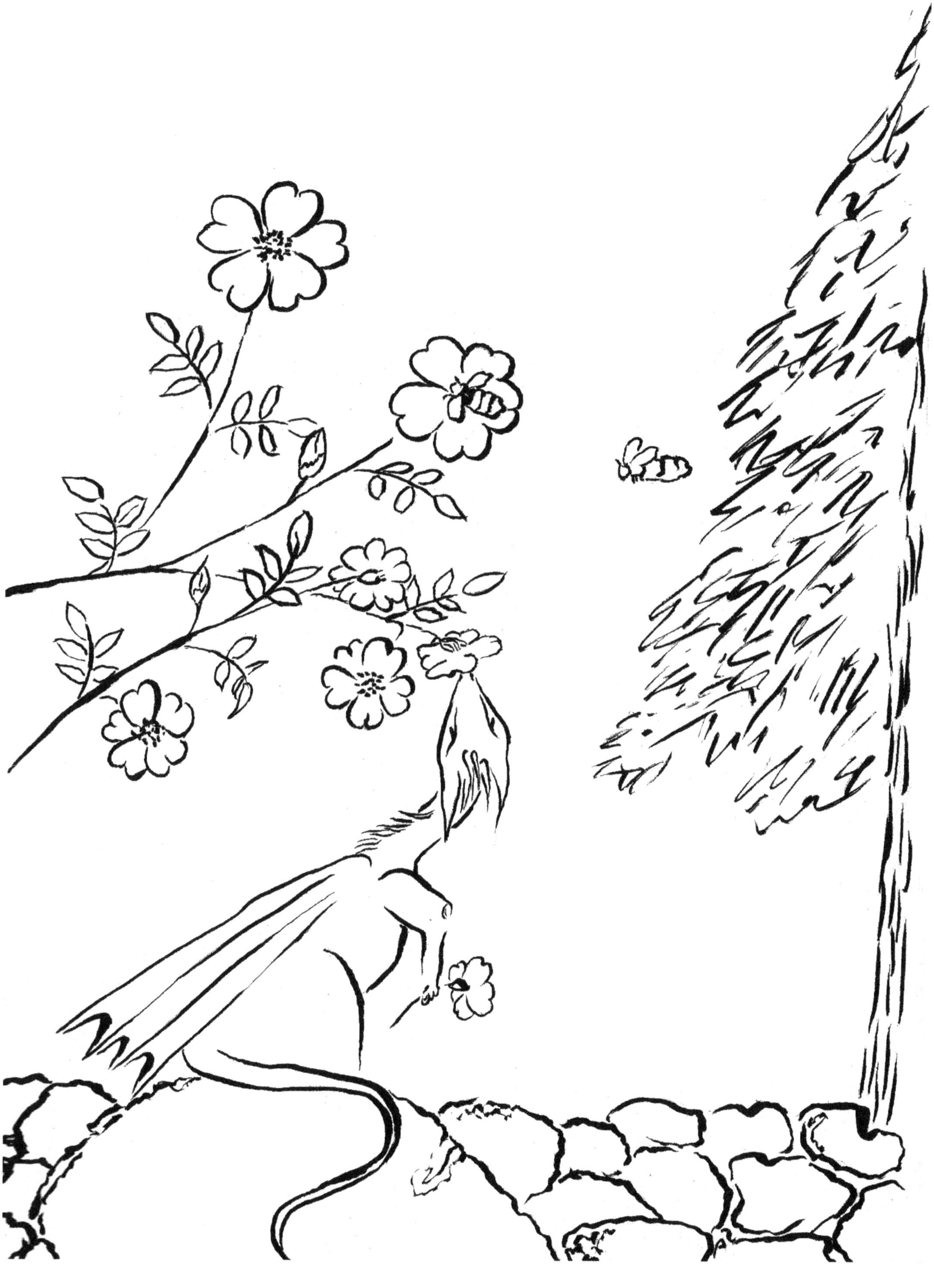

While Coloring, Add backgrounds, or details, to
make the pages your own.

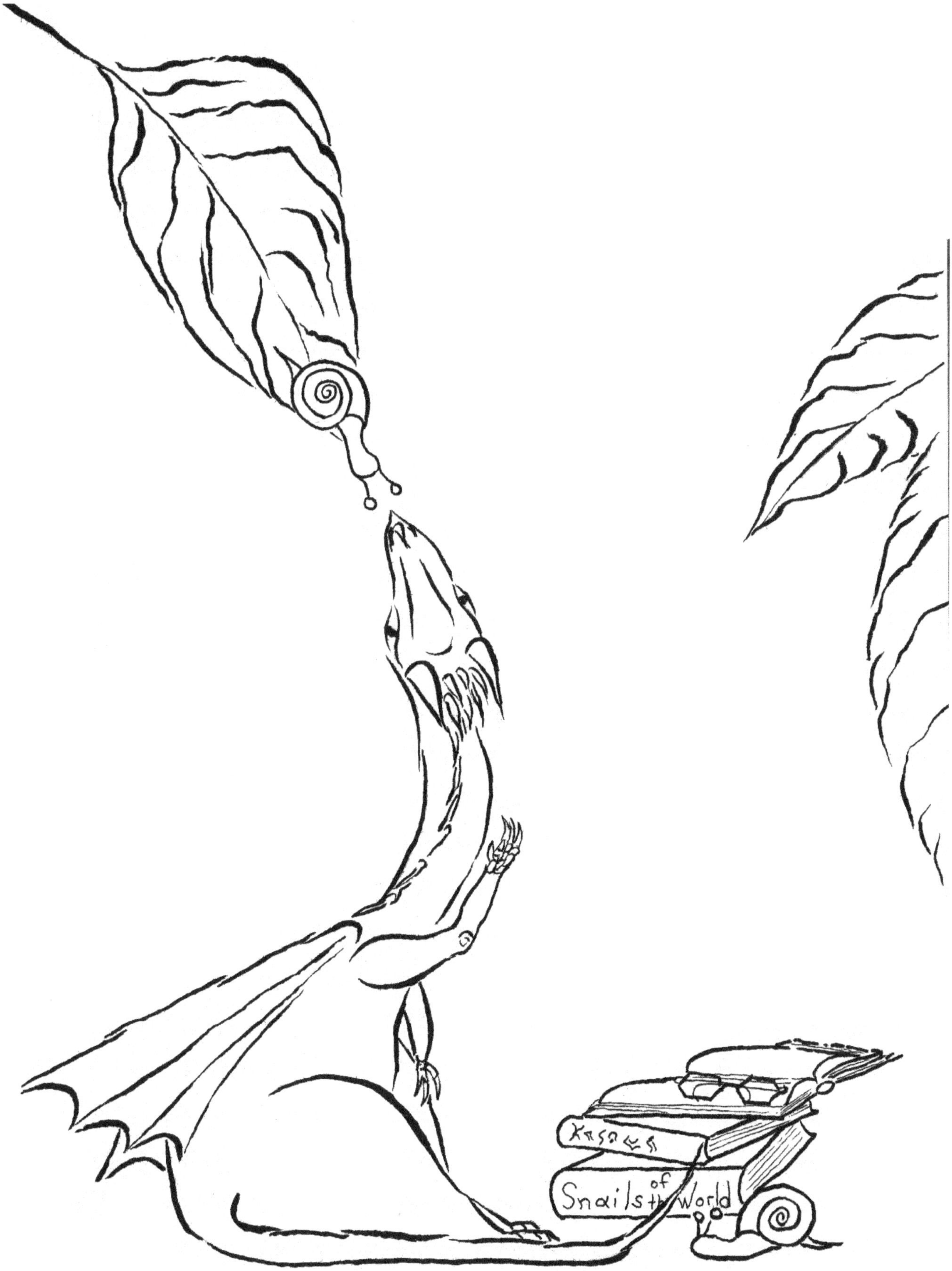
Snails of the World

The Lowly Snail

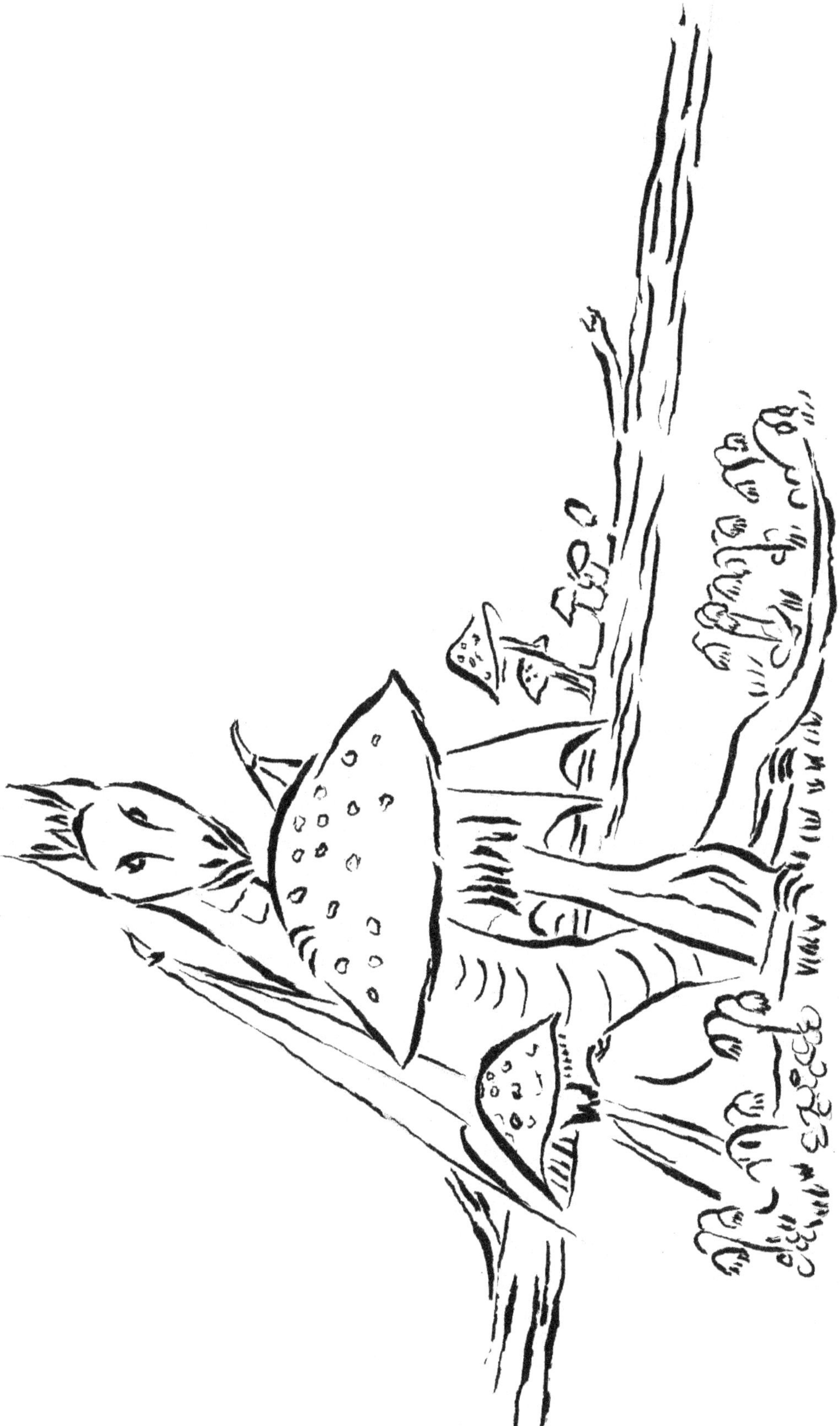

DODECATHEON PULCHELLUM

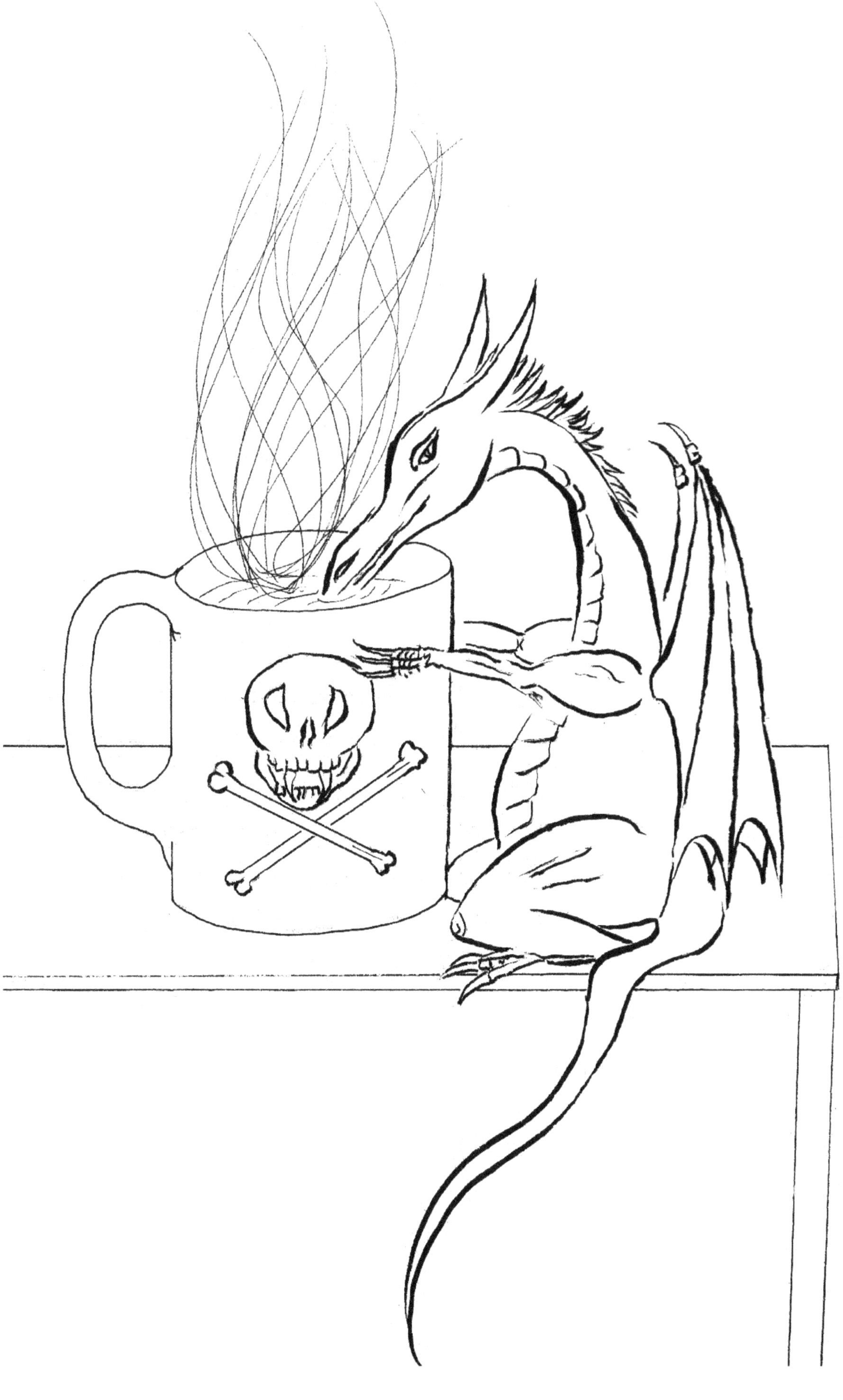

LADYSLIPPER ORCHIDS ARE A DELICATE PINK

BUBBLES! MAD SCIENCE IS BUBBLY

ROUGH MORNINGS NEED COFFEE

BETTA FISH

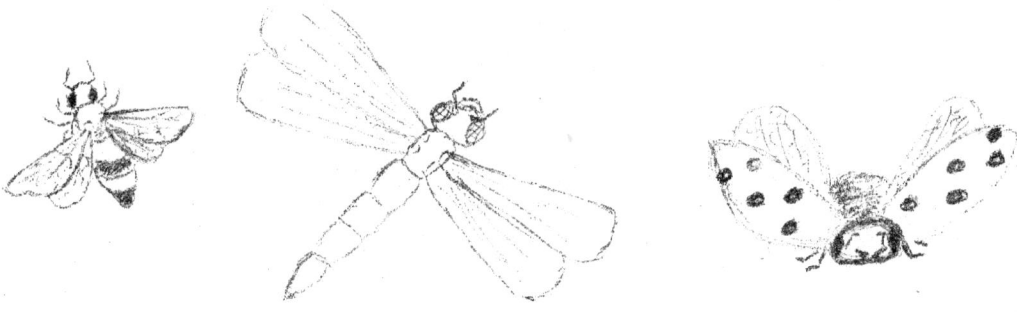

MEADOW DENIZENS

CAT
AND
DRAGON

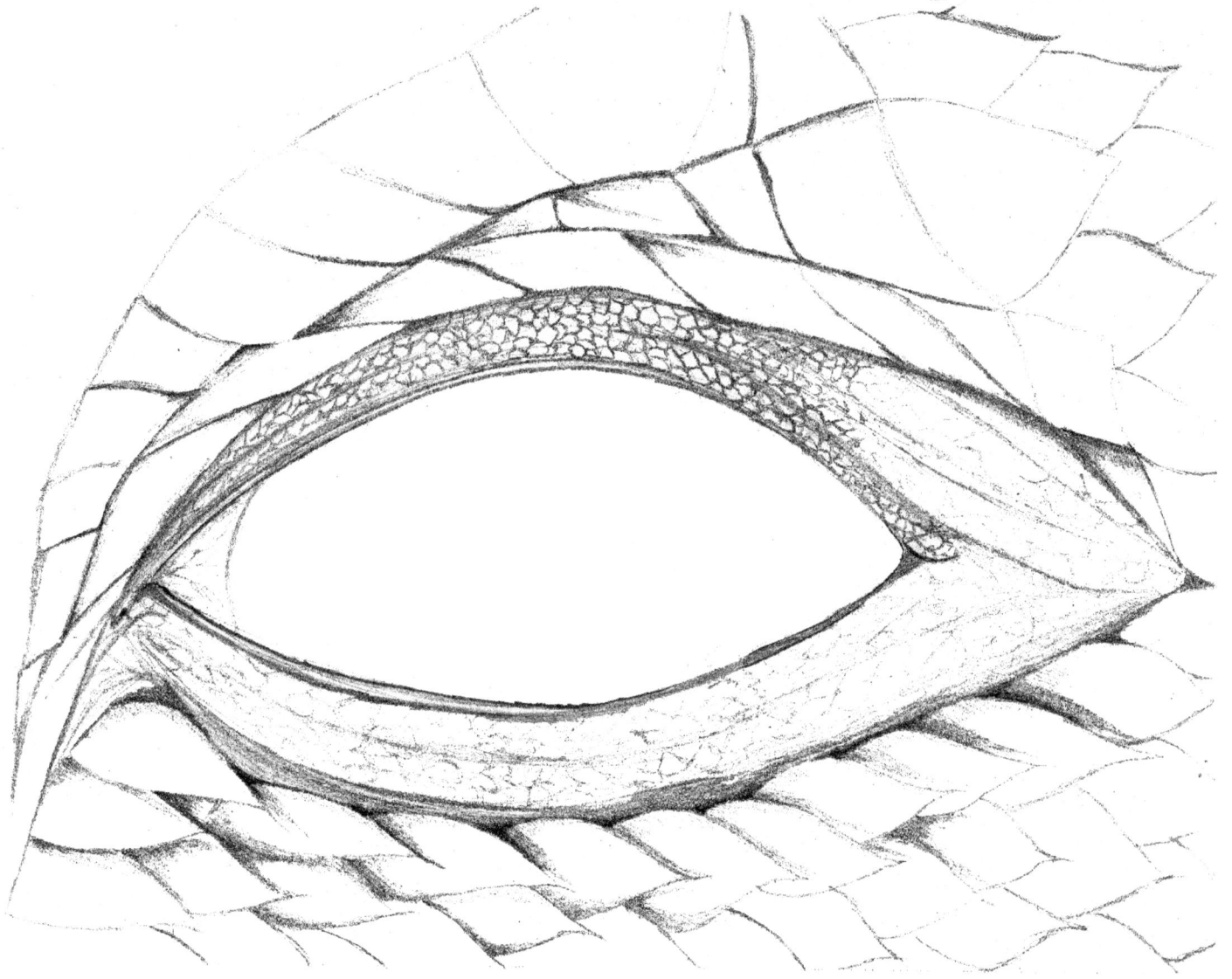

Dragon's Eye

The rest is up to you, you are the pupil.

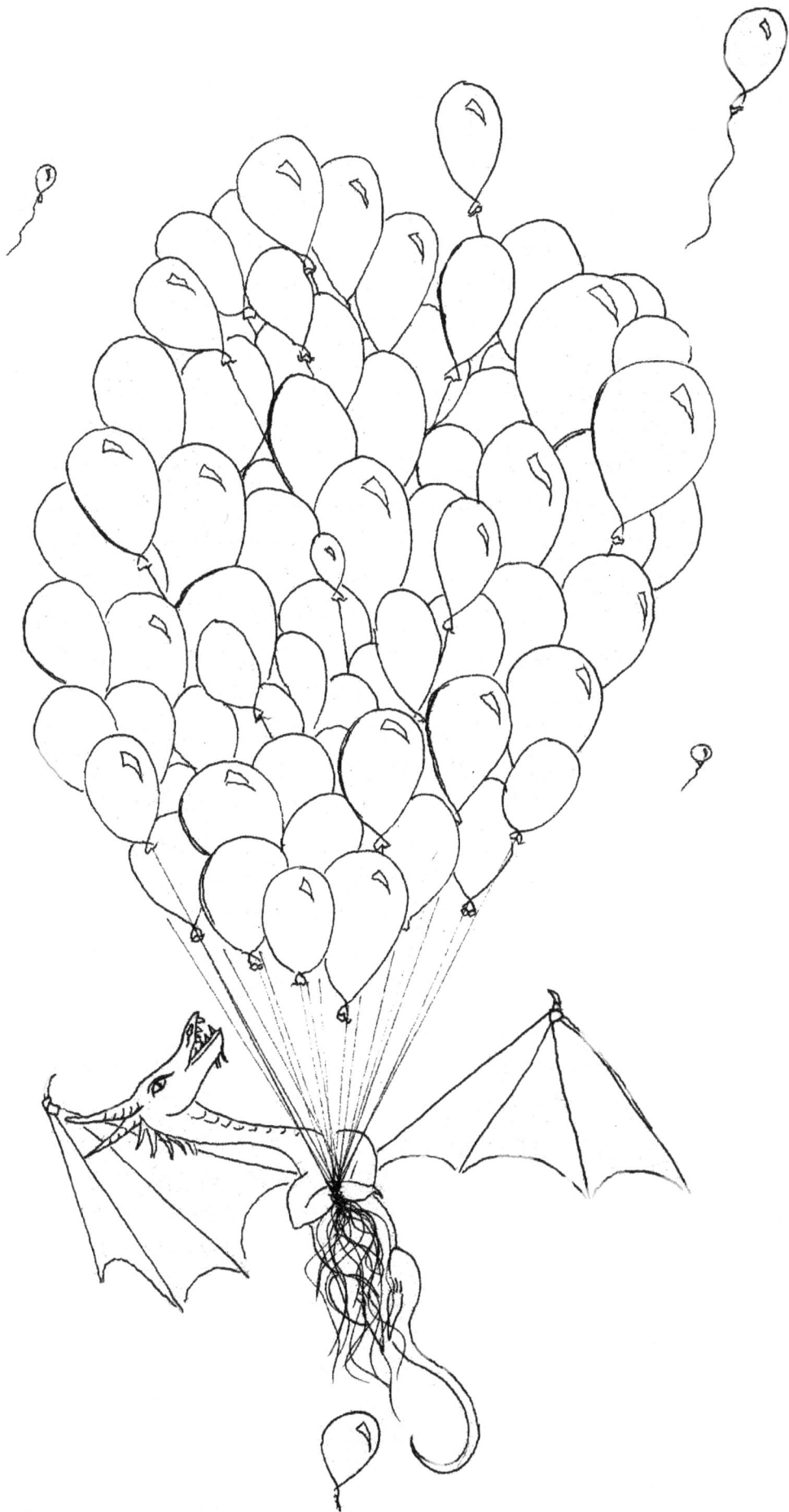

Give me back my wings...

I AM NOT A PET!

EVERY LIBRARY
NEEDS A DRAGON

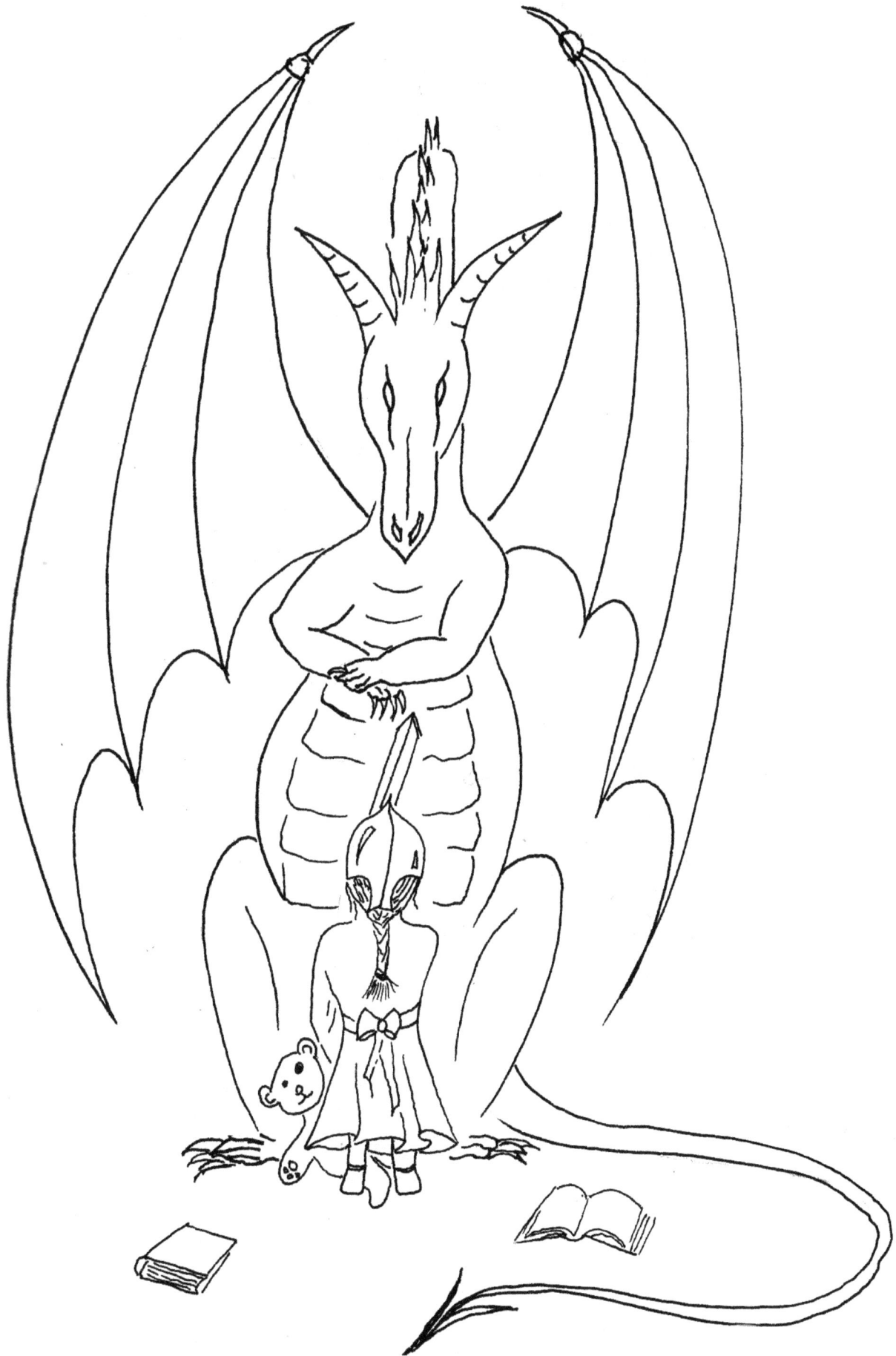

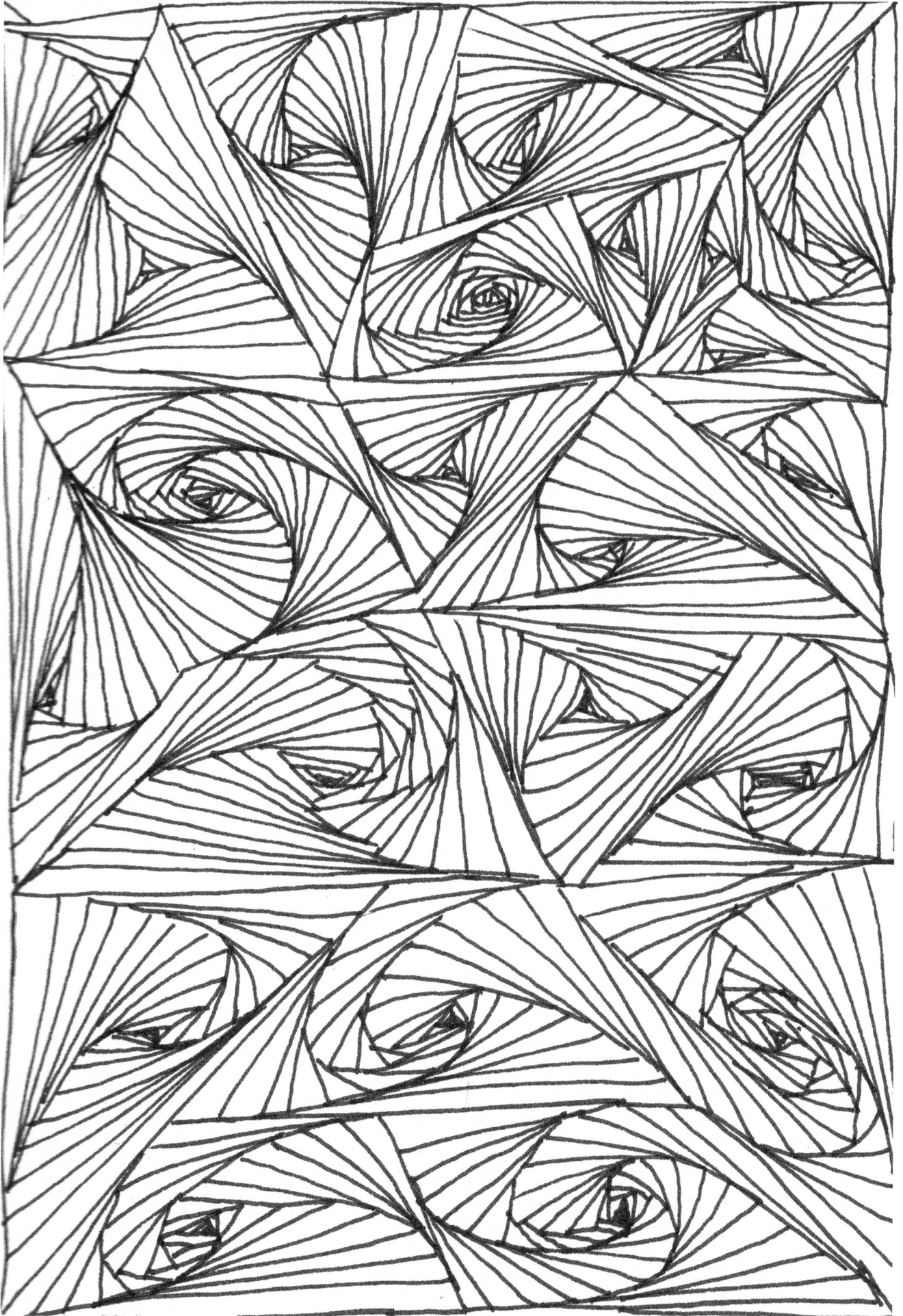

The Optical illusion is for my daughter, who asked for one.

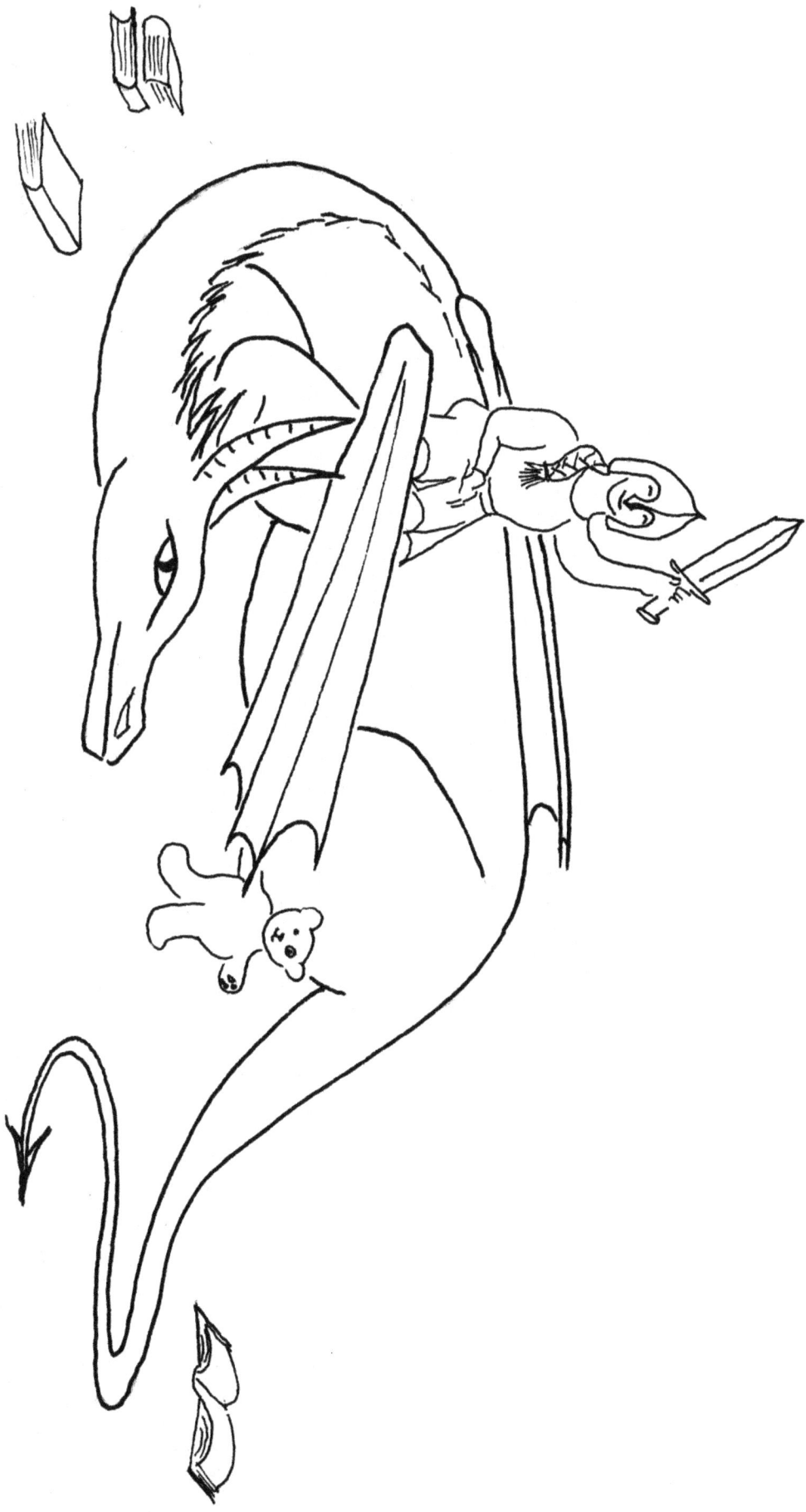

KITTEN CUDDLES

DRAGON DREAMS

HOW TO DRAW A DRAGONS

Cedar's way

I tend to draw dragons – anything, really, as minimally as possible. A few lines, a suggestion, a hint, and the viewer's brain does that cool thing we call closure. The human mind extrapolates from what it is given and interprets it on an unconscious level. This is how we see shapes in clouds. But the baby dragons I created a little more detailed than, say, my zen kitty.

I like to begin with the eyes. Eyes define the character of a drawing. Especially when you are cartooning like these characters, they can be the defining point of what the dragon is feeling, and that starts the story in the mind of the viewer. Cartoony eyes are great, and endlessly varied. I've done a few here just for ideas, not all dragon eyes, and you can look up eyes for many more ideas. Draw your own in the empty space, then let's begin.

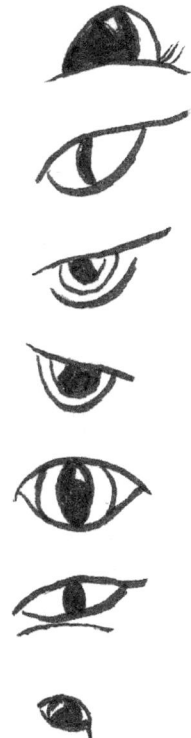

The first step is to sketch the basic shapes of the dragon.
The head is an oval and a triangle, the
body is a long S-shape with extra if
you want a longer tail. The wing is a
sort of triangle – the more acute your triangle,
the more closed and relaxed the wing.

The next step is to start adding details, still
with a soft pencil. I like to use a drawing
pencil that I know I will be able to erase cleanly, later.

You will see that as I'm
details, I am also changing
suit the little character as he
I'm not fully drawing
dragon in profile with
leg, and wing
Napoleon pose
hard and you will want

sketching more
some of the underlying shapes to
reveals himself.
him, this is a
his other arm,
hidden. Also, in
because hands are
to work up to them.

Finally, I ink the little
body shape and details
here the faint pencil lines
usually like a brush pen
variation to line weight,
coloring book illustrations
more static single pen.
I will erase all the pencil
in software that allows me to
finally have a line-art file with a
can be used to print on paper.

dragons, further refining
when I do so. You can see
under the pen. I
to give some
but many of the
were done with a
Once I'm done here,
marks, scan it, edit
remove all the back ground and
transparent background that
Perfect for coloring!

DRAGONS RULE!

www.ingramcontent.com/pod-product-compliance
Lightning Source LLC
Chambersburg PA
CBHW081659270326
41933CB00017B/3223